BOOSEY & HAWKES PIANO EDITIONS

T0069368

BÉLA BARTÓK

The First Term at the Piano

EDITED BY IMMANUELA GRUENBERG

Includes access to online video piano lessons
with editor Immanuela Gruenberg addressing
topics in Bartók's *The First Term at the Piano*.

To access companion video piano lessons online, visit:
www.halleonard.com/mylibrary

Enter Code
6692-6052-7677-2382

Cover Art: Linda Nelson

Videographer: H. Paul Moon, Zen Violence Films (zenviolence.com)

ISBN 978-1-4950-9125-4

BOOSEY &HAWKES

DISTRIBUTED BY

HAL•LEONARD®

Copyright © 2017 by Boosey & Hawkes, Inc.
International Copyright Secured All Rights Reserved

For all works contained herein:
Unauthorized copying, arranging, adapting, recording, internet posting, public performance,
or other distribution of the music in this publication is an infringement of copyright.
Infringers are liable under the law.

www.boosey.com
www.halleonard.com

World headquarters, contact:
Hal Leonard
7777 West Bluemound Road
Milwaukee, WI 53213
Email: info@halleonard.com

In Europe, contact:
Hal Leonard Europe Limited
1 Red Place
London, W1K 6PL
Email: info@halleonardeurope.com

In Australia contact:
Hal Leonard Australia Pty. Ltd.
4 Lentara Court
Cheltenham, Victoria, 3192 Australia
Email: info@halleonard.com.au

RELATED ONLINE VIDEO PIANO LESSONS

No. 1: Moderato
Lesson 1: The Big Picture

No. 2: Moderato
Lesson 2: Articulation

No. 3: Dialogue (Moderato)
Lesson 3: Getting from White to Black Keys

No. 4: Dialogue (Moderato)
Lesson 4: Playing Marcatissimo
Lesson 5: Different Touches Played Simultaneously

No. 5: Moderato
Lesson 6: Slur and Staccato Combination

No. 6: Moderato
Lesson 7: Shaping a Semi-Static Line

No. 7: Folksong (Moderato)
Lesson 8: A Beautiful Alberti Bass

No. 8: Andante
Lesson 9: The Choreography of Imitation

No. 9: Andante
Lesson 10: Dynamic Independence of the Hands

No. 10: Hungarian Folksong (Allegro)
Lesson 11: Back and Forth and Forward and Back

No. 11: Minuet (Andante)
Lesson 12: "Wrist Staccato"

No. 12: Swineherd's Dance (Allegro)
Lesson 13: Staccato and Sustained Notes
Played Simultaneously

No. 13: Hungarian Folksong (Andante)
Lesson 14: Avoiding the Beat Trap
Lesson 15: Same Key, Different Fingers
Lesson 16: Playing Two Notes Together

No. 14: Andante
Lesson 17: Melodic Syncopations

No. 15: Wedding Song (Moderato)
Lesson 18: Changing Fingers on Repeated Notes

No. 16: Peasant Dance (Allegro moderato)
Lesson 19: A Variety of Touches

No. 17: Allegro deciso
Lesson 20: Alternating Staccato and Tenuto

No. 18: Waltz (Tempo di Valse)
Lesson 21: Subtle Balance Between Melody
and Accompaniment

The price of this publication includes access to companion video piano lessons online,
for download or streaming, using the unique code found on the title page.
Visit **www.halleonard.com/mylibrary** and enter the access code.

PAGE

4 COMPOSER BIOGRAPHY

5 HISTORICAL AND PEDAGOGICAL COMMENTARY

7 ABOUT THE RELATED ONLINE VIDEO PIANO LESSONS

8 LESSON PLANS ON THE INDIVIDUAL PIECES

17 ABOUT THE EDITOR

THE FIRST TERM AT THE PIANO

18 No. 1: Moderato

18 No. 2: Moderato

19 No. 3: Dialogue (Moderato)

19 No. 4: Dialogue (Moderato)

20 No. 5: Moderato

20 No. 6: Moderato

21 No. 7: Folksong (Moderato)

21 No. 8: Andante

22 No. 9: Andante

23 No. 10: Hungarian Folksong (Allegro)

24 No. 11: Minuet (Andante)

24 No. 12: Swineherd's Dance (Allegro)

25 No. 13: Hungarian Folksong (Andante)

26 No. 14: Andante

26 No. 15: Wedding Song (Moderato)

27 No. 16: Peasant Dance (Allegro moderato)

27 No. 17: Allegro deciso

28 No. 18: Waltz (Tempo di Valse)

The price of this publication includes access to companion video piano lessons online,
for download or streaming, using the unique code found on the title page.
Visit **www.halleonard.com/mylibrary** and enter the access code.

Béla Bartók was born in the Hungarian town of Nagyszentmiklós (now Sînnicolau Mare in Romania) on 25 March 1881, and received his first instruction in music from his mother, a very capable pianist; his father, the headmaster of a local school, was also musical. After his family moved to Pressburg (now Bratislava in Slovakia) in 1894, he took lessons from László Erkel, son of Ferenc Erkel, Hungary's first important operatic composer, and in 1899 he became a student at the Royal Academy of Music in Budapest, graduating in 1903. His teachers there were János Koessler, a friend of Brahms, for composition and István Thoman for piano. Bartók, who had given his first public concert at the age of eleven, now began to establish a reputation as a fine pianist that spread well beyond Hungary's borders, and he was soon drawn into teaching: in 1907 he replaced Thoman as professor of piano in the Academy.

Béla Bartók's earliest compositions offer a blend of late Romanticism and nationalist elements, formed under the influences of Wagner, Brahms, Liszt and Strauss, and resulting in works such as *Kossuth*, an expansive symphonic poem written when he was 23. Around 1905 his friend and fellow-composer Zoltán Kodály directed his attention to Hungarian folk music and, coupled with his discovery of the music of Debussy, Bartók's musical language changed dramatically: it acquired greater focus and purpose – though initially it remained very rich, as his opera *Duke Bluebeard's Castle* (1911) and ballet *The Wooden Prince* (1917) demonstrate. But as he absorbed more and more of the spirit of Hungarian folk songs and dances, his own music grew tighter, more concentrated, chromatic and dissonant – and although a sense of key is sometimes lost in individual passages, Bartók never espoused atonality as a compositional technique.

His interest is folk music was not merely passive: Bartók was an assiduous ethnomusicologist, his first systematic collecting trips in Hungary being undertaken with Kodály, and in 1906 they published a volume of the songs they had collected. Thereafter Bartók's involvement grew deeper and his scope wider, encompassing a number of ethnic traditions both near at hand and further afield: Transylvanian, Romanian, North African and others.

In the 1920s and '30s Bartók's international fame spread, and he toured widely, both as pianist (usually in his own works) and as a respected composer. Works like the *Dance Suite* for orchestra (1923), the *Cantata profana* (1934) and the *Divertimento* for strings (1939), commissioned by Paul Sacher, maintained his high profile; indeed, he earned some notoriety when the Nazis banned his ballet *The Miraculous Mandarin* (1918–19) because of its sexually explicit plot. He continued to teach at the Academy of Music until his resignation in 1934, devoting much of his free time thereafter to his ethnomusicological research.

With the outbreak of the Second World War, and despite his deep attachment to his homeland, life in Hungary became intolerable and Bartók and his second wife, Ditta Pásztory, immigrated to the United States. Here his material conditions worsened considerably, despite initial promise: although he obtained a post at Columbia University and was able to pursue his folk-music studies, his concert engagements become very much rarer, and he received few commissions. Koussevitzky's request for a *Concerto for Orchestra* (1943) was therefore particularly important, bringing him much-needed income. Bartók's health was now failing, but he was nonetheless able virtually to complete his Third Piano Concerto and sketch out a Viola Concerto before his death from polycythemia (a form of leukemia) on 26 September 1945.

by Immanuela Gruenberg

Béla Bartók was one of the most important and most influential composers of the twentieth century. He was also a busy and successful concert pianist and teacher. In addition, as an ethnomusicologist, Bartók studied and researched the folk music of several countries, primarily that of Hungary.

Bartók composed more piano works than any other twentieth-century composer. These compositions include a large number of pedagogical works.

BARTÓK'S STYLE

Bartók's early compositions were influenced by the music of composers from the Classical and Romantic periods. Later compositions show influences of his contemporaries—Debussy, Schoenberg, and Stravinsky. The rise of Hungarian nationalism also influenced Bartók's style and his ethnomusicological work. His training in the classical style and his love of peasant music resulted in a style that is a synthesis between the two.

In contrast with some of his predecessors, among them his compatriot Liszt, Bartók did not use elements of gypsy music as representative of Hungarian folk music. His source of inspiration was the Hungarian peasant and Bartók incorporated into his classical compositions various elements of that music: motives, rhythms, scales, and the structures of various folk songs.

Nationalism wasn't the only reason Bartók turned to folk music for inspiration. He also preferred, and therefore sought out, unembellished, non-exaggerated, objective, and "pure," music. Bartók stated that "… peasant music continually inspires the composer. [...] if one hears songs from peasants in their original environment, one understands them much better; they inspire him much more than if he were familiar with them only from written collections or recordings." [1]

BARTÓK THE TEACHER

Bartók was very much interested in the art of piano teaching. He was professor of piano at the Budapest Academy for twenty-seven years. He also prepared many pedagogical publications. Some of these were teaching editions of standard classical works: Bach's *Well-Tempered Clavier*, piano sonatas by Scarlatti, Mozart, Haydn, and Beethoven, various works by Schubert and Chopin, and so on. Other publications were pedagogical compositions by Bartók himself. These include sets such as *Mikrokosmos*, *Ten Easy Pieces*, and *The First Term at the Piano*.

SZ

Sz stands for Andras Szöllösy who, in 1957, introduced a numbering system identifying Bartók's works and writings.

INTERPRETING BARTÓK'S PERFORMANCE NOTATIONS

Adapted from Benjamin Suchoff's *Guide to the Mikorkosmos*, pp. 22–25

Touch

Staccato: The duration of the note can range from shortest to no more than half the note's value.

Legato: The notes should be connected, but not overlapping.

Legatissimo: An exaggerated *legato*, with slight overlapping of tones. Use of half pedal is helpful.

Tenuto: A weighted touch that creates a stress and gives the note a special color. Notes marked *tenuto* should be held for their full rhythmic value.

Portato: Indicated by *staccato* signs under a slur. Similar to *staccato-tenuto* but played with a light, non-weighted, touch.

Accents

Accents are proportional to the surrounding dynamics. For example, *sf* in a *p* passage is softer than *sf* in a *f* passage.

Sforzato (**sff**, **sf**): The strongest possible accent.

Marcatissimo (^): Less strong than *sforzato*; it is a stress "of an agogic, emphatic, espressivo character."

Marcato (>): An accent that is weaker than *marcatissimo*.

Syncopations are played with some weight and emphasis.

Dynamics

A dynamic sign is in effect until replaced by another.

The second of two slurred notes should be softer than the first.

THE FIRST TERM AT THE PIANO

In 1912, Béla Bartók and Sandor Reschofsky, his colleague at the Budapest Academy of Music, started to collaborate on a publication called *Piano Method*. The plan was to publish several volumes, arranged by level of difficulty, from beginner through advanced levels. *Piano Method* included exercises and etudes, and compositions that matched the etudes' specific technical issues and their levels of difficulty. According to Reschofsky, he and Bartók agreed to not specify who contributed what to that publication. It appears that Reschofsky wrote the exercises and etudes while Bartók composed the corresponding pieces. The first volume of *Piano Method* (Sz. 52) was published in 1913.

In 1929 Bartók published *The First Term at the Piano*, Sz. 53. That publication consisted of 18 pieces Bartók extracted from *Piano Method*. These eighteen pieces correspond to the following numbers in *Piano Method*: 21, 22, 24, 26, 36, 40, 44, 51, 59, 68, 77, 89, 95, 105, 116, 115 (in that order), 118, 119.

It is interesting, though probably not surprising, that the *Piano Method* starts off with ear training and singing (basic solfège). Singing these little pieces should be an integral part of learning them. This is also good ear training for the student.

Note to teachers: Not included in *The First Term at the Piano* are those pieces and exercises from *Piano Method* that help the student transition from one level to the next. In the discussion of the individual pieces, I identify the main new skill(s) that each piece focuses on, in order to make it easier to learn these skills before, or immediately upon, assigning a new piece.

Tempo and Metronome Markings

Numbers 1–7 are marked Moderato, but note Bartók's wide range of metronome markings for that one tempo: from quarter note = 52 to quarter note = 96. Upon closer examination we see that the faster metronome applies to pieces where the shortest rhythmic values are quarter notes and the slower metronome markings, to pieces with eighths notes.

Fingering

All fingerings are by the composer.

General practice tips

The following tips apply to all the pieces in the set.

- Play and sing each hand's part.
- Play hands together and sing one, then the other part.
- Play one part and sing the other. This can be challenging!
- Sing from memory.
- If the left-hand part is too low to sing, move the piece up an octave; if the right-hand part is too high, move the piece down an octave.
- See if you can write down the piece—from memory.
- Always, always shape the lines, whether they are *legato*, *portato*, or *staccato*.
- Practice hands together with the left hand playing *piano* and the right hand playing *forte*. Then reverse.

The online video piano lessons included with this publication are intended for both teachers and students. They address a variety of pianistic and artistic issues and how these relate to Bartok's piano music. In designing these lessons, I've focused on the most important or most obvious technical and musical elements of these eleven pieces while also aiming to cover a wide range of topics. That said, please bear in mind that due to their brevity, these lessons only offer a sample of the many technical and musical challenges and possibilities found in these little pieces, all of which should be addressed.

As with all types of lessons, you are encouraged to apply relevant suggestions offered in one lesson to pieces discussed in another. For example, the video lesson **Articulation** for piece No. 2 pertains to most of these pieces, wherever articulation is called for. Likewise, lesson No. 6, **Shaping a Semi-Static Line** can be easily applied to No. 9 (both the right and the left hand), and to Nos. 10 and 18. You may use these video lessons on their own, but they are most beneficial when combined with the performance suggestions in the Historical and Pedagogical Commentary and the Lesson Plans on the Individual Pieces.

—Immanuela Gruenberg, editor and video piano lesson teacher

by Immanuela Gruenberg

No. 1: Moderato
ABOUT THIS PIECE

- Hands together, parallel motion, five-finger position
- Phrases: Each is three measures long
- Quarter, half, and whole notes
- Stepwise motion
- *f* should be interpreted as playing with a full tone. This is important for young students whose hands and fingers aren't very strong. That said, the student should never force the tone.

PRACTICE TIPS FOR THE STUDENT

- Look at measures 1–3. See if you can play and/or sing the melody. Now do the same with measures 4–6.
    - Did you notice something interesting?
    - Do these two phrases have anything in common?
    - What is the word that describes how these two relate to one another? (Answer: "sequence")
- Play the first phrase, sing the second (without playing it), play the third, and sing the fourth. Then reverse the play/sing order.
- Make sure to play *legato* and to breathe in between phrases.
- To achieve *legato*, "roll" the weight from one finger to the next.
- Look at the shape of the phrases. Each has a beginning, middle, and end. Try to make your playing follow that shape.
- Measures 9 and 12: Count four beats and keep your counting steady. No rushing!

No. 2: Moderato
NEW IN THIS PIECE

- Phrases of varying lengths
- Counterpoint: More independence of the hands, playing in parallel and in contrary motion. Also different rhythms for each hand.
- A variety of rhythms consisting of quarter notes, half notes, whole notes, dotted half notes, and rests.

PRACTICE TIPS FOR THE STUDENT

- The *f* dynamics should be interpreted as playing with a full tone.
- Note: measures 9–12 are a repeat of measures 1–4.
- Measure 13 is slightly different from measure 5. Make sure that your playing shows that.
- With a pencil, draw the shape of each hand's line:
    - Where do the two hands play in parallel?
    - Where do they move in opposite directions?
    - Play the right while your teacher plays the left-hand part, then switch.

No. 3: Dialogue (Moderato)
NEW IN THIS PIECE

- Five-finger position, but different keys for each hand
- Black keys
- *p* dynamics
- 3/4 meter
- Counterpoint: dialogue of independent hands imitating one another

- Hands breathe independently, each at a different place
- Beginnings and endings of phrases do not coincide
- The *p* dynamic and the 3/4 meter give this piece a gentler and a more flowing character compared to the previous pieces in this collection.

PRACTICE TIPS FOR THE STUDENT

- Bartók named this piece Dialogue (a conversation between two or more people). Before you start playing the piece, take a look at the music and think about the following:

  Can you tell what makes this piece a dialogue?

  How many participants are in this dialogue?

  Do they agree or disagree with each other?

  Who among the participants expresses multiple ideas and who repeats more of the same?

- Even though it is marked *p*, practice hands together with one hand playing *p* and the other *f*. This helps each hand to gain independence. Focus especially on playing the right hand *p* and the left hand *f*, to make sure that the left hand does not "hide" behind the right.

- Note that on several occasions one "person" waits and listens to the other:

  Measures 4 and 8: release the right-hand C on time!

  Measures 5 and 9: the left hand is quiet, listening to what the right hand has to say.

  Measure 13: release the left-hand G-sharp on time

- Pay special attention to measures 12 and 15. In both cases the left hand continues its *legato* line while the right hand has to breathe.

No. 4: Dialogue (Moderato)

NEW IN THIS PIECE

- *Marcatissimo* (^)
- Different touches (*marcatissimo* and *non-marcatissiomo*) played simultaneously by both hands
- Ties

PRACTICE TIPS FOR THE STUDENT

- Both thumbs are on C, one octave apart.
- In this piece you can clearly see the difference between a tie and a *legato* indication.
- Measures 2–3 and 13–14: the right hand continues its *legato* line while the left hand breathes.
- Carefully count that first long note. Even more important is for you to listen to it! Listen how the sound slowly decays. Play random long notes on the high, middle, and low parts of the keyboard and listen to their slow, perfect diminuendos.
- Measures 5, 7, and 14: both hands play on the downbeats, but only the left hand is marked *marcatissimo*. Practice these notes first, focusing on the different touches.

No. 5: Moderato
NEW IN THIS PIECE
- Slow tempo
- *Staccato*
- Playing *legato* with both hands, *staccato* with both hands, and also *legato* with one hand and *staccato* with the other (mm. 6–7)
- Eighth notes

PRACTICE TIPS FOR THE STUDENT
- This piece contains parallel motion (mm. 1–4) and contrapuntal motion (mm. 6–8).
- Measures 1–4: let the strong fingers (1 and 2) of one hand guide the weaker fingers (4 and 5) of the other, but don't let them hide these fingers. Think of the strong fingers as the conductor.
- The slow tempo and *forte* dynamics mean that this piece should sound very rhythmic. Be in control of the tempo!
- Look at measures 6–7. Here the composer makes the piece just a tad trickier, right? Playing *legato* with one hand and *staccato* with the other means that you have to carefully practice first hands separately and then hands together.
- Measure 6: play the first note of both hands, making sure that the right-hand B is *staccato* and the left-hand G is held
- Play measure 5 and stop on the first note of measure 6. Now go on to the next beat and do the same.
- Practice the first two beats of measure 6. Pay attention to how the *staccato* and *legato* feel, and listen to how they sound.
- Now add the third beat of that measure, making sure that the left hand plays a *staccato* D while the right hand holds down the A.
- While playing this, listen to the left-hand line that ends on the *staccato* D.
- Once you've mastered measure 6, practice measure 7 the same way.

No. 6: Moderato
NEW IN THIS PIECE
- Slow, lulling tempo
- Right-hand melody against left-hand accompaniment
- More complex combinations of previously introduced elements:
    Lines of varying lengths
    Right-hand articulation versus left-hand *legato*
    Rests
    Long notes
    Ties

PRACTICE TIPS FOR THE STUDENT
- The repetitive patterns make this piece easier. Still, there are many details you need to pay attention to.
- Play measures 1–4 in tempo. What is the character of this piece? What does it feel like? Does it remind you of anything? Maybe it's a lullaby, with its constant lulling, rocking motion. Or maybe a hurdy-gurdy with its repetitive, droning accompaniment.
- If you are also learning No. 5 in this collection, can you compare the *staccatos* in the two pieces?
- Measures 6 and 8: savor the mirror image!
- Measure 10: Don't play the downbeat, but make sure you count it!
- Maintaining a slow tempo isn't easy. Imagine rocking a baby to sleep. You have to keep it slow and *piano*, otherwise the baby will wake up!

No. 7. Folksong (Moderato)

NEW IN THIS PIECE

- Dynamic changes
- Echo effect
- Alberti-like accompaniment
- Two-note (long-short) slurs
- Articulation, *legato*, *staccato*, rests—all, against a *legato* left hand
- Both hands in five-finger position in F major (but only the left hand plays B-flat so there's no fourth finger on a black key)

PRACTICE TIPS FOR THE STUDENT

- Measures 3–4 are an echo of measures 1–2; measure 6 is an echo of measure 5.
- Take the contrasting dynamics very seriously. Your listeners have to be able to tell that you're switching back and forth between *f* and *p*.
- Measures 1 and 3: right-hand eighth notes should be released gently, even when playing *forte*. This is different from the *staccatos* in measures 2 and 4.
- Measure 2: With a pencil, draw a line that connects all the notes of the left-hand part, just like you play Connect the Dots. Look at that line and try to "draw" its shape with your playing.
- Play the left-hand part, leaving out the repeated Fs. What have you got? You have the melody, a sixth below the right hand, hidden within this Alberti-like pattern. So make sure to shape the left-hand part, especially the beautiful lines in measures 2 and 4.

No. 8. Andante

NEW IN THIS PIECE

- Andante (rather than moderato)
- Crescendo and decrescendo, *sf*, *marcato* (>)
- Canon-like opening and polyphony

PRACTICE TIPS FOR THE STUDENT

- With a pencil, mark the places where the right and left hands play very similar material? Find as many such instances as you can.
- Now let's look at some less obvious instances:

    Measures 8 (second half) and 9: Both hands play the exact same pattern—same notes, one octave apart—starting a beat apart.

    Measure 10 (second half): right plays B-G-A-C while the left hand plays G-B-C-A, reversing the first two and last two notes.

- Measures 2–3: each *sforzando* should be louder than the previous one, as they are all part of the crescendo.
- Remember: both hands are equally important.

No. 9. Andante
NEW IN THIS PIECE

Playing simultaneously, *p* with one hand and *f* with the other

PRACTICE TIPS FOR THE STUDENT

- Note the contrasting dynamics: left-hand *f* and right-hand *p* in measures 1–4; reversed to left-hand *p* and right-hand *f* in measures 5–8; again reversed back in measures 9–12.
- Look at the left hand in measures 1–4 and the right hand in measures 5–8. Are these melodies related? If you think they are related, can you tell how, and in how many ways they are related? (Answer: mm. 5 and 7 are a reverse of mm. 1 and 3. mm. 6 and 8 are also very similar.)
- Practice a few times with the hands two or three octaves apart. This makes it easier to distinguish between the two hands/voices.
- Play the *piano* parts softly but don't forget to shape the lines.

No. 10: Hungarian Folksong (Allegro)
NEW IN THIS PIECE

Harmonic intervals—seconds, thirds, and fourths—played with one hand

PRACTICE TIPS FOR THE STUDENT

- Practice the left hand as blocked, three-note chords. Play one chord per measure. Do this with the left hand alone and also with the right hand playing its part as written.
- When playing the left hand as written, move it left and right, in a seesaw motion. Note that the thumb always plays alone while finger 5 always plays with one other finger: 4, 3, or 2.
- Starting at measure 5, the back and forth motion in the left hand contains an inner "voice:" G–A–B-flat–A. Listen to it and shape the line.
- Listen to the long lines and shape them. Measures 5–8 are a question and measures 9–12, an answer. Likewise, measures 13–16 and 17–20.

No. 11: Minuet (Andante)
In *Piano Method*, this minuet is preceded by "Swineherd's Dance" (No. 12 in the present collection).
NEW IN THIS PIECE

- Right hand covering two-plus octaves; left hand covering a tenth
- The hands stretch wider than a five-finger position
- Double sixths
- Relatively long series of *staccatos*
- Grazioso: a subtle but specific character indication

PRACTICE TIPS FOR THE STUDENT

- If you have never before played sixths, play this interval now. Listen to what it sounds like. Pay attention to what it feels like in your hand.
- A "minuet" is a noble, stately, elegant dance. It should never feel rushed or be too loud. Look at pictures and maybe watch some video clips of people dancing a minuet.
- *"Piano grazioso"* means that the piece is to be played lightly, with a wrist *staccato*.
- Note that even after a four-measure crescendo, it never gets louder than *mf*.
- Please pay attention to the different touches: *staccato* (on its own or with *marcato*); *tenuto*; two-note slurs.
- Perform the accents within the context of the dynamics (*p*) and the character (*grazioso*). Think of the accents as gestures that add grace to the music. They should never sound aggressive.
- Make sure your wrists are supple, relaxed.
- To reach the interval, let the hand fall open, never force-stretch it.

No. 12: Swineherd's Dance (Allegro)

NEW IN THIS PIECE

- Two voices, and different touches, played simultaneously by one hand
- Five-finger position, transposed

PRACTICE TIPS FOR THE STUDENT

- This is a relatively easy example of playing two voices with one hand. Preparation exercises can consist of any two-note chords (or series of chords) in which one note is held while the other is quickly released.
- Play each hand's part with two hands. That way, you can more easily control each "voice" and teach your ear to distinguish between them.
- Practice the *staccato* melodies only, hands separately. Then practice the *staccato* melodies hands together, still without the long notes. Pay attention to the difference between *staccato* and slurred notes. Think long lines: a four-measure question and a four-measure answer.
- In measures 1–8, fingers 5 are anchors; also in measures 10–16. These stay in place while other fingers move.
- Once you have played an anchor note, make sure you do not lean too hard on it or push down on it. Very little weight is needed to keep these keys down.
- *Marcatissimo* (^) and *sf* in a *piano* passage are softer than they are in a *forte* section.

No. 13: Hungarian Folksong (Andante)

This piece is based on an actual Hungarian folk song, among the ones collected by Bartók in 1912.

NEW IN THIS PIECE

- Double thirds
- Hands traveling on the keyboard by means of changing fingers on repeated notes
- Single line transferred between the hands (mm. 7 and 8)

PRACTICE TIPS FOR THE STUDENT

- Measures 1–8: make sure that the downbeat really does sounds like a downbeat and not like an upbeat. This is a bit tricky because the long notes in the measure fall on weak beats, and the left hand has a rest on the downbeat.
- Keep the left hand *legato* when the right hand articulates, and vice versa.
- Measures 7 and 8, fourth beat: the left-hand D is part of the accompaniment and the melody. Make a nice *legato* from the right-hand F-sharp to E to the left-hand D.
- Measures 10–16: shape the left-hand line. The repeated Ds should be softer than the melodic notes.
- Measures 1–8, left hand: make sure that the two notes of the chords are played together.

No. 14: Andante

In *Piano Method*, this piece is written in the key of G, not F.

NEW IN THIS PIECE

- Polyphony
- Syncopated melody
- *Sempre legato*

PRACTICE TIPS FOR THE STUDENT

This piece is quite similar to Bach's Invention in E Major, BWV 777. Same syncopated voices, similar scale-like lines, and similar second motive.

- Make sure you play really *legato*, as Bartók indicated.
- If the first time around you bring out one voice, on the repeat try to bring out the other.
- Play hands separately several times in order to hear and to remember what each of the voices sounds like.
- Measures 5–9: plan a gradual, controlled diminuendo from **mf** in measure 5 to **p** in measure 9. To do so, play measure 5 and the beginning of measure 6 **mf**. Then play measure 9 **p**. And now, fill in that "space:" play measure 7 a soft **mf** and measure 8 **mp**, with a diminuendo to **p** in measure 9.

No. 15: Wedding Song (Moderato)

NEW IN THIS PIECE

- A variety of chords, consisting of two, three, and four notes
- *Non-legato* touch includes thumb-under and hand-over-thumb
- *Pesante*
- Very specific tone/touch indications. Every single note and every single chord has a special marking, either *tenuto* or *staccato*. All, in addition to *f* and *pesante*.

PRACTICE TIPS FOR STUDENTS

- Look at measures 1–6. Note that all chords, except for one (m. 3, beat 5), are marked *tenuto*. The left-hand (melody) notes that coincide with these chords are also marked *tenuto*.
- Now look at measures 7–12. Here the chords are played by the left hand and are marked *staccato* (again, with one exception: beat 2 in m. 7). The right-hand notes that coincide with theses chords are *tenuto*. In other words, in measures 1–6, *tenuto* coincides with *tenuto*, and in measures 7–12, *tenuto* coincides with *staccato*.
- Pay close attention to these details, but keep in mind the long lines, long musical phrases.

No. 16: Peasant Dance (Allegro moderato)

NEW IN THIS PIECE

- *Alla breve* (cut time)
- Accented syncopations
- Hand crosses over and under thumb in *legato* passages

PRACTICE TIPS FOR THE STUDENT

- Note that the syncopations in measures 2, 4, 6, and 8, are all marked *marcatissimo*.
- The left-hand slurs divide each measure into two equal parts, in line with the alla breve meter.
- In a two-note slur, the second note should be softer and slightly shorter than the first. Since in this piece the second note stays the same throughout the piece, it makes all the more sense to play it softer.
- Repetitive material should never sound repetitive. Note the following minor changes in repeats:

    Measures 1–2 form a question, and measures 3–4 are the answer.

    In measures 5–6, we hear a similar, but not identical question. The answer to that question (mm. 7–8) has more authority because of the left-hand *staccato* chords in measures 7–8. Make sure your playing shows these differences.
- This piece combines a precise beat and strong accents, with beautiful melodic lines. Observing the *legato* in measures 1, 3, 5, and 7 is important in demonstrating these twin qualities.

No. 17: Allegro deciso

NEW IN THIS PIECE

- More complex rhythms
- A variety of chords, from seconds to sixths, including double sixths played simultaneously by both hands
- *Allegro deciso* requires a strong rhythmic sense and a firm hand and finger.

PRACTICE TIPS FOR THE STUDENT

- Observe the specific touch notations that Bartók included for every single note or chord (compare to No. 15).
- Begin by clapping the rhythm. Make sure the beat is very steady.

No. 18: Waltz (Tempo di Valse)

NEW IN THIS PIECE

- Tempo: This is the fastest piece in the set
- Subtle dynamic differences between melody (*mp*) and accompaniment (*p*)
- *Portato*: right hand, measures 9–20

PRACTICE TIPS FOR THE STUDENT

- In a waltz, beats two and three are lighter than the downbeat, so make sure the *staccatos* are light and gentle ones.
- Try to show the difference between the questions (mm. 1–2, 5–6, etc.) and the answers (mm. 3–4, 7–8, etc.). These sentence should end with a "musical period."
- Remember, this is a dance, so after you've done all the careful practicing, have fun playing the piece and your listeners will enjoy it, too.

Endnotes

[1] Schneider, An Interview, in *Laki*, Bartók and his World, 230.

[2] Suchoff, *Piano Music of Béla Bartók*, series II, p. xxiii.

For Further Reading

Antokoletz, C., Fischer, V., and Suchoff, B, ed. *Bartók Perspectives*. Oxford and New York: Oxford University Press, 2000.

Bartók, Béla. *Essays*. Benjamin Suchoff, ed. New York: St. Martins Press, 1976; Lincoln and London: University of Nebraska Press, 1992.

Bartók, Béla and Reschofsky, Sándor. *Kalvierschule*. Budapest: Editio Musica Budapest, 1913; German translation 1943; revised German translation 1964.

Chalmers, Kenneth. *Béla Bartók*. London: Phaidon Press Limited, 1995.

Cooper, David. *Béla Bartók*. New Haven and London: Yale University Press, 2015.

Crow, Todd, ed. *Bartók Studies*. Detroit: Detroit Reprints in Music, 1976.

Demeny, Janos, ed. *Béla Bartók Letters*. London: Faber, 1971.

Gillies, Malcolm. "Bartók, Béla." *Grove Music Online. Oxford Music Online*. Oxford University Press. www. oxfordmusiconline.com

_____. *Bartók Remembered*. New York: W. W. Norton & Company, Inc., 1991.

_____, ed. *Bartók Companion*. Portland: Amadeus Press, 1994.

Kovács, Sándor. "The Ethnomusicologist." in *The Bartók Companion*, edited by Malcolm Gillies. Portland: Amadeus Press, 1994.

Laki, Peter, ed., trans. *Bartók and his World*. Princeton: Princeton University Press, 1995.

Schneider, David E. *Bartók, Hungary, and the Renewal of Tradition*. Berkeley, Los Angeles, London: University of California Press, 2006.

Sipos-Ori, Robert. *A Performer's Guide to Bartók's Ten Easy Pieces and Allegro Barbaro*. Koln: Lambert Academic Publishing, 2009.

Stevens, Halsey. *The Life and Music of Béla Bartók*. Oxford: Clarendon Press, 1993.

Suchoff, Benjamin. *Béla Bartók: A Celebration*. Lanham, Maryland, and Oxford: Scarecrow Press, Inc., 2004.

_____, ed. *Béla Bartók Essays*. Lincoln and London: University of Nebraska Press, 1992.

_____. *Guide to the Mikorkosmos*. Silver Spring: Music Services Corporation of America, 1965.

Yeomans, David. *Bartók for Piano*. Bloomington: Indiana University Press, 1988.

Immanuela Gruenberg is a pianist, teacher, lecturer, and editor. She has appeared in concerts and presented workshops and master classes in the United States, South America, Israel and the Far East. Critics described her performances as "supreme artistry" (*Richmond News Leader*) and as "lyrical and dramatic" (*Buenos Aires Herald*). She has performed in venues that include the Chamber Series of the Israel Philharmonic, the Jerusalem and Tel Aviv Museums; Buenos Aires' Classical Radio and Israel's Classical Radio, the Kennedy Center, Corcoran Gallery, Strathmore Mansion, and the Smithsonian Museum's "Piano 300" series, celebrating the 300th anniversary of the invention of the piano. Other "anniversary" performances include lecture recitals in the United States and in Israel on Schubert's posthumously-published piano sonatas—the topic of her doctoral dissertation— in honor of the composer's bicentennial anniversary, and a performance of Josef Tal's Concerto for Piano and Electronics, in honor of the composer's 85th birthday. She has presented lectures on piano performance, piano literature, and pedagogy at venues such as the World Piano Pedagogy Conference, the National Conference on Keyboard Pedagogy, various MTNA chapters, colleges and universities, as well as for the general public. Critics lauded her "highly intelligent program notes" and praised her for speaking "intelligently about each piece" (*The Washington Post*). She has taught master classes at the Central Conservatory in Beijing, China, and the Liszt Academy in Buenos Aires, Argentina, among other places.

Dr. Gruenberg is editor and recording artist of several publications in the *Schirmer Performance Editions* series and for Boosey and Hawkes, published by Hal Leonard. *Clavier Companion* review said that *"Beethoven: Easier Piano Variations* is a must for any instructor's library…. informative commentary, helpful practice suggestions, and wonderful recording…" and *American Music Teacher* praised her "thoughtful fingering" and that she "offers helpful but not dogmatic suggestions about style and interpretation" and provides "a wealth of information about 18-century performance practices and variation form." Her edition of *Bartok: Ten Easy Pieces* was praised as "highly valuable to piano students, teachers and Bartok scholars alike" (*American Music Teacher*), while a *Clavier Companion* review said that "Immanuela Gruenberg creates a real gem… a must-have for any teaching library… her short video demonstrations may set the standard for literature books going forward."

Immanuela Gruenberg served as chair of the Washington International Competition, was a member of the editorial committee of *American Music Teacher* journal, is a member of the National Conference on Keyboard Pedagogy's Committee on Independent Music Teachers, and is Vice-President for Programs for MCMTA.

A magna cum laude graduate of Tel Aviv University's Rubin Academy of Music, she completed her Doctor of Musical Arts at the Manhattan School of Music in only two years. She studied piano with Professor Arie Vardi (for over ten years) and with Constance Keene, and chamber music with Boris Berman and Rami Shevelov. She also coached with Pnina Salzman and Thomas Schumacher. Dr. Gruenberg was a teaching assistant at the Manhattan School of Music in New York, a faculty member of the Music Teachers' College of Tel Aviv and the Levine School of Music in Washington, DC, and maintains an independent studio in Potomac, Maryland.

Related Online
Video Piano Lesson
1

The First Term at the Piano

Béla Bartók

Moderato (♩ = 96)

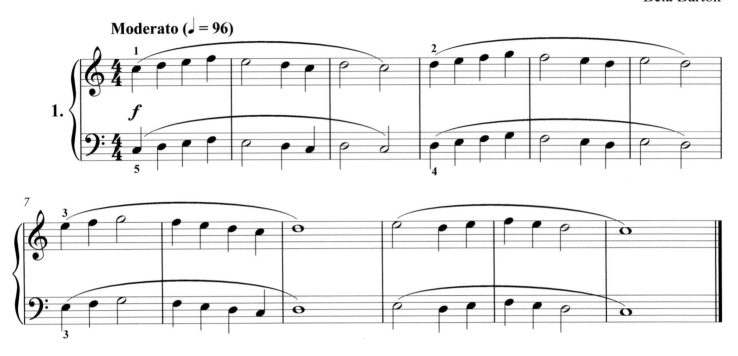

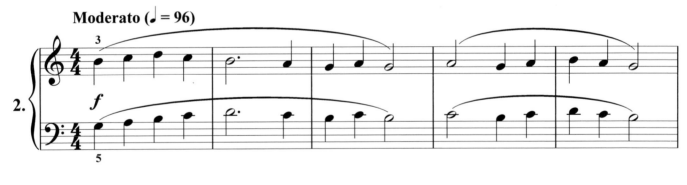

Related Online
Video Piano Lesson
2

Moderato (♩ = 96)

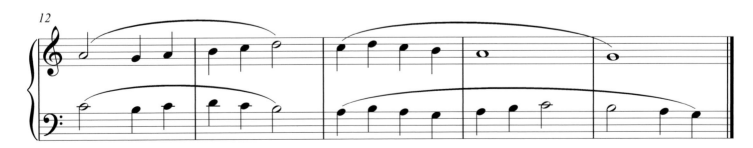

Copyright © 2017 by Boosey & Hawkes, Inc
International copyright secured.   All rights reserved.

Dialogue

Related Online
Video Piano Lesson
3

Related Online
Video Piano Lessons
4 and 5

Dialogue

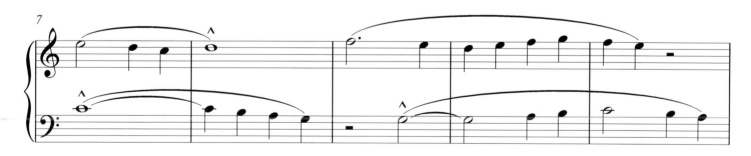

Related Online
Video Piano Lesson
6

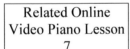

Related Online
Video Piano Lesson
7

Folksong

Related Online
Video Piano Lesson
8

Related Online
Video Piano Lesson
9

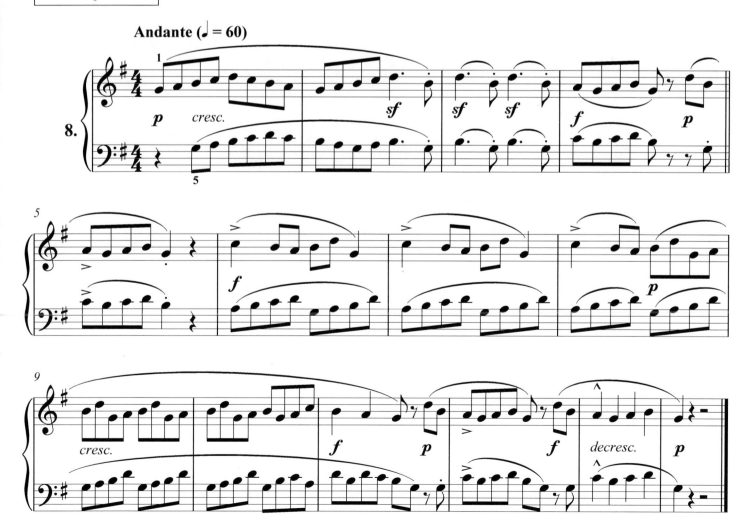

Related Online
Video Piano Lesson
10

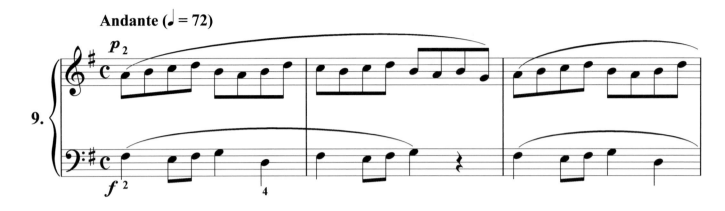

9.

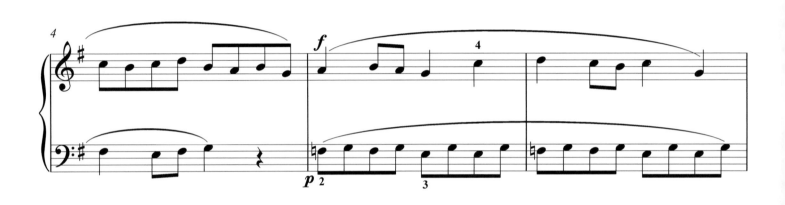

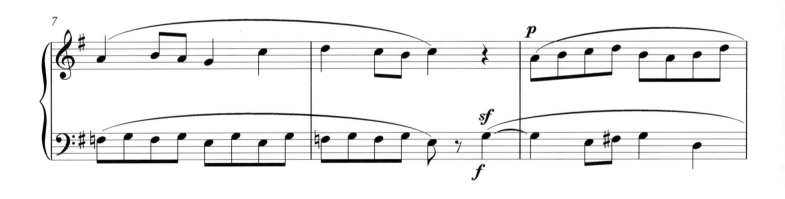

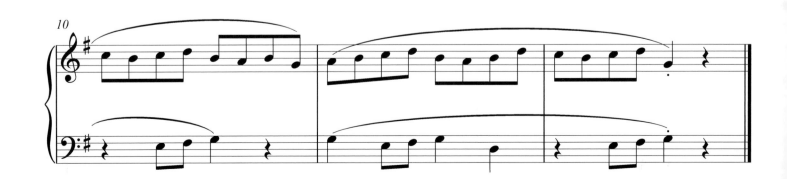

Hungarian Folksong

Related Online
Video Piano Lesson
11

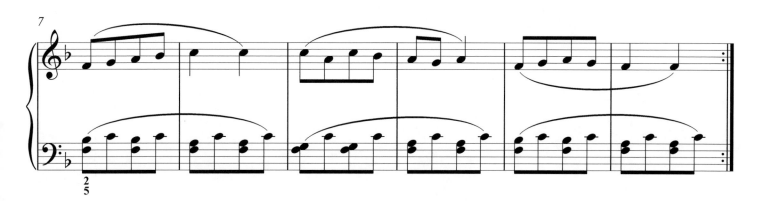

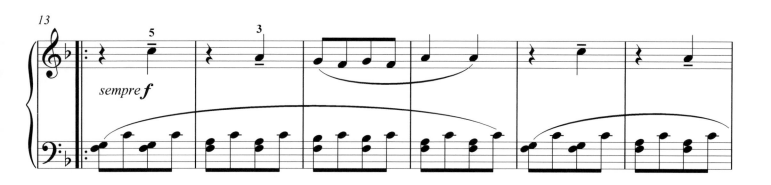

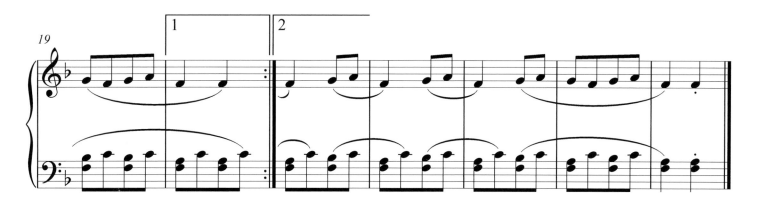

Minuet

Related Online
Video Piano Lesson
12

Related Online
Video Piano Lesson
13

Swineherd's Dance

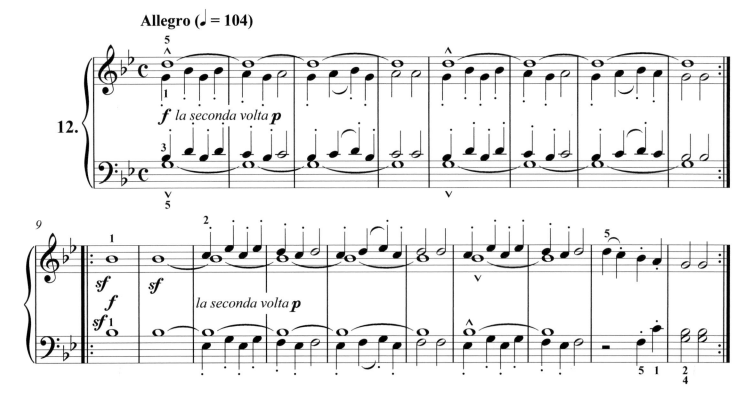

Related Online
Video Piano Lessons
14, 15, and 16

Hungarian Folksong
(Where Have You Been, Little Lamb?)

Andante (♩ = 80)

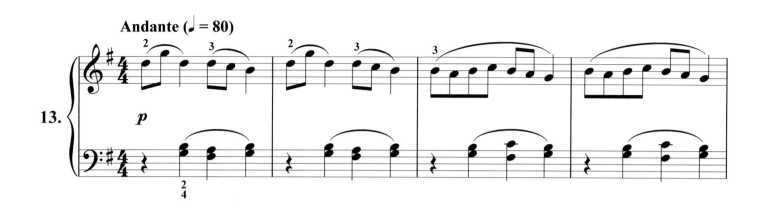

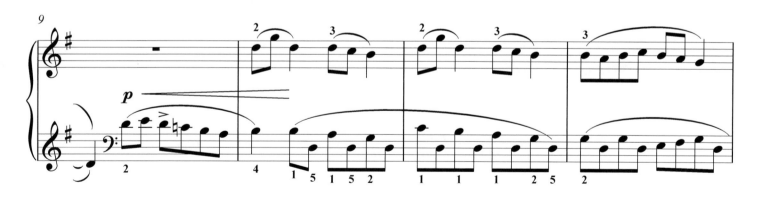

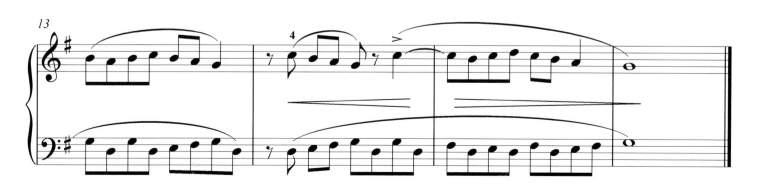

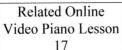

Wedding Song

Peasant Dance

Related Online
Video Piano Lesson
19

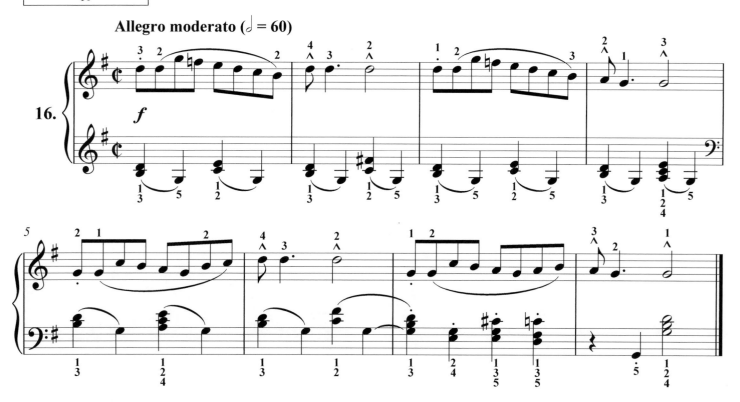

Related Online
Video Piano Lesson
20

Related Online
Video Piano Lesson
21

Waltz

Tempo di Valse (♩ = 116)

18.

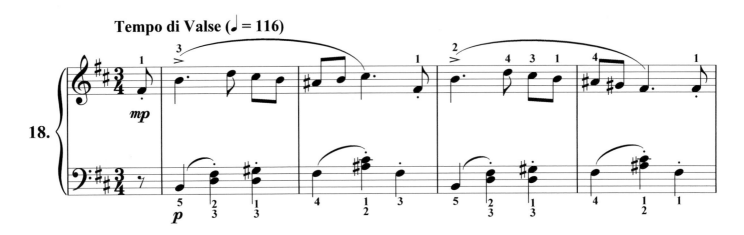

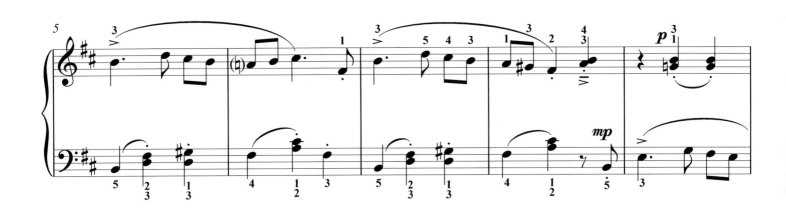

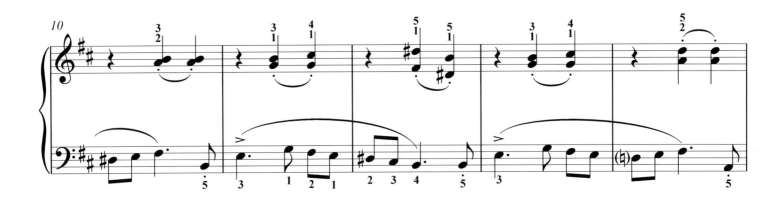

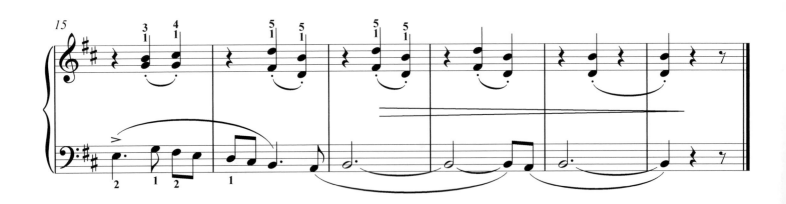